Advance Praise for *Slack Tongue City*

"Poet from Louisville, KY, Mackenzie Berry has accomplished a grand task with her first book, *Slack Tongue City*— one of taking us readers home, of placing us wholly there. A love letter to her city, find in these poems: food, fried green okra and $23 sandwiches, love and critique, childhood nostalgia and unwavering solitude, family and the interior—history, history, history. No one is left out of Berry's heartache for her hometown, not those that frown upon hearing the city's name, not those on the margins of its history. No one, for even the ghosts are angels, for even 'a ghost / alives' her 'past tense.'"

> **—Hajjar Baban**, author of *What I Know of the Mountains*

"'There's no way out of the South but driving.' In the urban pastorals of *Slack Tongue City*, the landscape for this coming-of-age is Louisville in all its biscuit and eggs wonder. 'When the heart stops, the chest bursts upward like a sky split endless.' Lyrical in its hard-won authority, clear-eyed in its portrayal of Southern life, *Slack Tongue City* reminds us that no matter where we are, through the twin forges of witness and love, we 'can still hear the sea.' A percussive debut."

> **—Quan Barry**, author of *We Ride Upon Sticks*

"Mackenzie Berry's *Slack Tongue City* sings a texture of voices in the everyday tension between the communal and the personal. Shaped by the poet's upbringing in Louisville, Kentucky, this debut shakes the branches of childhood, neighborhood, family, and grief—those evergiving trees —the fruits of which Berry has, without a doubt, transformed into art, through musical and vivid poems. 'I show you where I'm from & you don't change it,' the poet writes. Berry is a gifted storyteller weaving rhythm, formal range, and startling tenderness into this irresistible invitation to the 'front porch / or at least a stoop.' If you have ever wondered how to hold your people and places of origin in your heart in all their complexity, *Slack Tongue City* is for you."

    —**Oliver Baez Bendorf**, author of *Advantages of Being Evergreen*

"If ever a hometown was a character, Louisville fits the bill. Mackenzie Berry boldly explores the eccentricities of her birthplace in her electric debut, *Slack Tongue City*. So aware of the curiosity of it all, the poet insists there must be a metaphor for 'how the Midwest is at the nape of our neck huddling us into a hallway on a Thursday but the South knocks like a rock thrown at the door on Sunday morning.' *Slack Tongue City* is, in fact, that figure of speech: twisting, turning, and refusing to be anything other than free."

    —**Mitchell L. H. Douglas**, author of *dying in the scarecrow's arms*

"Berry's sentences spiral through the layers of Louisville, uncovering what is hidden beneath the trick of sight. The images spin, tunnel inside of themselves, singing as they go. Once you begin to follow Berry's winding path, you will feel the Slack Tongue City with more than your senses. Berry writes, 'Louhvul, the birth name in which the river fell South & unsung— // this begets the moment in which the tongue lilts, forever—the tongue— / that carries all the vowels heavy and slangs the weight slant.' Berry's poetry shows us how she bears this burden of history, the power of speaking— by allowing the syllables to 'lilt,' to 'slang,' and to 'slant' their way to remembering."

    —**Brandi George**, author of *Gog*

"Steel-eyed and tender, *Slack Tongue City* is a love letter to Louisville, to the South, to the multitude of selves contained in Mackenzie Berry's artful rendering of her beloved home. These poems do more than just bear witness—which they do—with Berry's careful precision, natural lyricism, and sly wit. Whether in lament or in praise, these poems sing with intimate knowledge of a Kentucky landscape and of her people: they testify, they pray, they spell-bind. And like truly good poems, they leave us hungry for more. This is a fierce and standout debut from a remarkable young poet, whose voice has already secured a place among a new generation of Southern writers. Mackenzie Berry is a force."

—Natasha Oladokun

Slack Tongue City

Sundress Publications · Knoxville, TN

ISBN: 978-1-951979-31-7
Library of Congress: 2022932355
Published by Sundress Publications
www.sundresspublications.com

Editor: Tennison Black
Editorial Assistants: Erin Elizabeth Smith, Kanika Lawton
Editorial Interns: Katy DeCoste, Neha Peri, Brooke Shannon, and Ryleigh Wann

Colophon: This book is set in Taviraj.

Cover Image: "Warning, Tried," by Katherine Watts

Cover Design: Kristen Ton

Book Design: Tennison Black

Author Photo: Daphne DiFazio

Slack Tongue City

Mackenzie Berry

Acknowledgements

The author extends gratitude to the following literary journals for publishing earlier versions of some of the poems in this collection:

Blood Orange Review: "On the Day I Bury the River"

Broadsided Press: "Song from the Color Red"

Hobart: "Biography of a [ ] Girl"

The Lumiere Review: "In Which an Entrepreneur is the Mayor"

StorySouth: "Jeff St. Baptist Community at Liberty" and "On Being From Nobody"

TAUNT: "3 Truths & a Lie"

Up the Staircase Quarterly: "My Mother Had Hands Before She Had Children" and "My City Saw the First Black Athlete Millionaire, Jockey Isaac Murphy, and Afterward the Winning Jockeys Were White"

Vinyl: "How a Temper Grows Up"

The poems "3 Truths & a Lie," "In Which an Entrepreneur is the Mayor," and "Every Summer a Garden Hose Made a Pool" were written in the writing workshop series, "Against Silence," taught by Joy Priest, organized through the Sarabande Writing Labs during the Louisville uprisings in summer 2020.

Contents

III.

for my hometown—my first love

I.

"All the Southerners think we're Yanks, and all the Yanks think we're Southerners, and all the Midwesterners think we're East. Everybody's always wrong about Louisville."

—Jim James

Tombstone for the Old Home

a mash-up of "My Old Kentucky Home" and Joy Priest's "Elegy for Kentucky"

The sun shines bright on my Old Kentucky home,

the same horse always dying at the curve.

The corn-top's ripe & the meadows lay toppled,

a filly done wide as all surrender.

For my Old Kentucky home, bred for offering,

welcome to finish its June-huge grief.

Weep no more my lady,

for that magnificent face still waiting for the end.

By 'n by hard times done before May's Derby

came the same way each evening, wanting.

For the old creature, any weak thing

can make music all the day.

The young roll throbbing, once-immortal

while we sing one song, far away.

Nowhere to drive to make sure it is still there

all merry, all happy & great belly.

I turned, for my Old Kentucky home,

still against the grass every time whispering—

Let's go. We are bright numb & done here, bridle.

Mom Said Louisville's not the South Because it Dresses Grits Fancy

Mom, from red clay pasture truck porch swing Georgia, said it's only the South if they had grits before they started dressing grits fancy. I, from hot brown Big Red river side Louisville, said Louisville's the South because you have to trip your tongue up to say it right. Mom, from the next house couldn't hear you if you screamed Georgia, said you can see Indiana from downtown so it's the Midwest. I, from tell me you didn't lick your fingers after you ate in my city Louisville, said Louisville's the South because the Ohio flows Mississippi. Mom, from the tea turns your blood molasses and twists your lips sour Georgia, said she planted the only magnolia tree in the city so it's the North. I, from bourbon isn't bourbon unless it's from Kentucky Louisville, said Louisville's the South because the city's spread out slow and the corner store clerks call everybody *honey*. Mom, said you can skip a rock to Indiana so it's not the South. I, said I'm not good at skipping rocks so it's the South. Mom, from cast iron fried green okra Georgia, said the overpriced Derby hats and mint juleps and plaid striped drunks are just a good show. I, from some orphan city of no swimmers, said Louisville's the South because it said so.

My City Saw the First Black Athlete Millionaire, Jockey Isaac Murphy, and Afterward the Winning Jockeys Were White

title after Frank X. Walker

Off Bayly, the train tracks split
the neighborhood like a highway,
steel & rust & picks in its teeth.
On one side, the bookstore, the library,
the breakfast spot with cinnamon rolls,
housemade. The other, Lee's Chicken, the diner,
the storefront that is always changing its name.
Portland, when it was its own town, was wealthy
before the wealthy left with the river traffic & now
the shotgun houses home huddled families,
the kids stashing syrup sandwiches for school,
hauling a backpack through a screen door past
a mother's reminder of shoes on the front porch.
The smoke shops send men
with Swisher Sweets behind their ears,
past monkey bars & red slides & a swing set
on the corner & the Seafood Lady,
food-truck-turned-staple, Kool-Aid in jugs

& shrimp mac & cheese. Off 9th Street,
the highway split the city like *Maniac Magee*,
Black Wall Street turned skyscraper & hotel.
The ripping is so ripe you can taste it.
The bricks, Sheppard Square & Cotter Homes
& Beecher, Indi's and King's with plexiglass
over the counter, faces obscured like a windshield.
Churches with lines around the block, drawn-faced men
and women shifting their weight from waiting.
Off 15th, the roads are one-way only, the buildings
closed up & shy, murals of faces & slant names
on the sides & parking lots made blacktops.
Garden beds raised on the in-betweens,
the Dirt Bowl Tournament, neighborhood squads
picking the rocks from their shoes & licking their hands,
the step teams & grill masters trading technique.
Way east, Indian Hills & Springhurst & Prospect,
where the buses don't go, lakes & streams & fountains,
picnic tables & willow trees & tee ball games.
It's like cleaning fish, this city, the head & eyes & spines
stripped clean to one side, all the meat to the other,
the hands doing the stripping swift & skilled & made to.

Jeff. St. Baptist Community at Liberty

Joe sings the Blues like he's calling
his children home / a rich oak deep velvet swoon
with enough cry to bend your knees and not collapse.
He sang a sermon in his overalls and the church said
Amen. He took his coffee black until he met
Goatwalker cream and then he took two spoons.
We here, who make pews of folding chairs
and make the bread stretch around the block,
have called this meeting begun by a reformed riverboat gambler
back when alcoholics were called drunkards
and we later called in all those sleeping in the stockyard's hay.
Once a woman walked in naked and our pastor didn't break scripture.
If I say too much, I might call the congregation awake,
all these rebel Southern Baptists who made it gay & misfit
and still call themselves—all these rich folks with empty pockets
and a leaky roof. What do you know of rising but what rose
down on Liberty St. the day God said let there be light and it poured?
I tell you, the Phoenix burned smiling for all we can make of ash.
The city comes for us flaming and eats itself to the marrow,
finds men sleeping in Sunday school rooms and rages,

spreads Clarksdale out across the city and leaves an empty lot,

where half of us still sit waiting for the grand return.

When the Association expelled us from Jefferson St.

for holding a woman pastor behind the pulpit,

we took an old factory building and made it hold us all

by the hand of an angel mechanic called Elmer,

and kept our name, too, but longer. Ate with the whole line

on 10 for 10 biscuits and eggs right next to Norma's House

after the steel-fist-in-a-velvet-glove woman called Mary

came and asked us what were we here for anyway.

I tell you, you haven't seen a party til Easter at Jeff. St.

when we dance on confetti just to see the mess splayed

and Di sneaks us the best piece. Gather us in,

where the prayer drums an open forum

of children too wild-eyed to call God *Mister*.

Contrapuntal in Which Ghosts are Actually Angels

I prefer a ghost

                                                 an angel never longs for me

                                                 & knows too well how to name my demons.

A ghost

                                                 the spirit of my shadow

alives my past tense.

Is a prayer not a haunting?

                                                 May be a ghost doesn't bless but asks forgiveness

                                                 from you.

What else can you call a thing that rises

                                                 from a cemetery?

Is a wail not the loudest holy in the room?

Does not all sacred come from the dead?

We kneel to ghosts

                                                 history is unborn

our clench softening, tithes paid

                                & flesh undone.

3 Truths & a Lie
[Louisville, Kentucky]

sometimes we see every season in a week & there must be a metaphor for the geographic battleground & tornado warning sirens & how the Midwest is at the nape of our neck huddling us into a hallway on a Thursday but the South knocks like a rock thrown at the door on Sunday morning & says remember it's hot like casserole like a church fan like pages clinging together like skin sticking to the pew like running sprints on the blacktop until all the body salt falls forehead to jaw & a cold shower is better than sleep. sometimes we see every season in a week like that one year the windstorm toppled the traffic lights like a beheading & then the snowstorm shuttered us in for two weeks & all the kids watched the bottom of the television screen & shouted for another lost school day until we didn't.

one time the bus never came.

it's the South because you have to have a car or be late.

it's the Midwest because it's in the river water.

one time we all cursed Indiana.

it's the South because segregation.

it's the Midwest because segregation.

if the library floods that's the same as defunding books.

if the city is a body it's redrawing its anatomy & cuts the left palm where the hip goes just to lie integration. if the city is a body it's redrawing its anatomy & cuts the colon where the throat goes just to say there's a new business district. if the city is a body it's redrawing its anatomy & cuts the fat where the lungs go so that both hands twist the torso and withdraw a clean red line.

one time i loved my city.

one time i critiqued it the most.

one time i shook my head in disgust

until i remembered all the houses & storefronts dissolving from my memory

once occupied & dissolved all the home from generation else's.

Sestina for Louisville Jug Band Music

> "These were the first of a string of recordings that would ignite a national jug band craze that would exhaust itself only during the Great Depression." —*Michael Jones*

Of all the histories, this one is the song of antebellum,

made into a record label minstrelsy after a Black birth.

Of all the vinyl, this one is the only Louisville band,

called Dixieland Jazz up from New Orleans by way of the Ohio River.

The jug band was born before the Depression,

sent down the Falls of the Ohio by a metal pie shell, 3 strings & a glass jug.

After Little Africa/West Parkland, the folk made the jug,

before it was made bastard & capital by the painters of Antebellum.

It filled the city after the Civil War, famed image of country depression.

Who witnessed a violin sax banjo washboard glass spoons birth?

The Good Old Days played the white buyers. Full as a river,

the Confederate influx kept the genres strict to the bands.

The spinners danced long enough to wave down the bands.

By marriage of vaudeville & ragtime, their miracle dirt child the jug,

McDonald and Hayes made the Original Louisville Jug Band & the Stompers chief of the river.

In this version, the jug doesn't sit at the rocking foot of the antebellum.

The Falls stilled boats & passerby into an overnight birth—
among the river traffic it is said that household items & brass jazz broke the depression.

Loud enough, the music pressed until the ground gave way to a depression.
West Africa brought the banjo to the Appalachia band,
which brought the jug song, lasting until the Civil Rights Movement birth.
The Victorian Age stage play where the hero wore blackface & played jug
swung on the front porches & wrote the hymns of American Antebellum
because it sold and the word reached the nation by way of the river.

The doula took her instruments and laid them at the base of the river.
When she soon followed depression,
knowing her light would be made a record of antebellum,
she tied the string tight at her belly not unlike the band,
who sat unsuspecting of all the stained glass windows they could jug.
In time, she took great care arranging the washtub bass birth.

To raise money for the house rent of the one who played the washboard birth,
the people gathered beneath the Second Street bridge at the river.
What of a revival if it is not an underground jug
where the shoulders give way deep as a sinkhole depression?
All the rest showed up because they were in the neighborhood band,
where the genesis was no gothic myth of antebellum.

The river cut through the romantic genocide of antebellum,
gave us the first jug, a throaty howl on the knee of a ragtag band,
held us through far more than an economic depression.

My Elementary School was Named After a Poet

for Coleridge-Taylor Montessori Elementary School

Across the street from the high school of Muhammad Ali,
a Louisville poet, my elementary school was named after
an English poet who died of pneumonia, no less.
His bio was Scotch taped to the hallway by the side stairs
and I read every sideline to avoid speaking.
The same school where in 3rd grade,
we read *so much depends upon / a red wheelbarrow*
and I wrote *so much depends upon / a park swing set*
because I didn't get the poem until Gavin wrote
so much depends upon / a yellow school bus—
but actually, so much does depend upon a park swing set,
which kept me from the sky, where I learned
feeling the wind is like flying standing still.
The first aircraft in space, the first feet to touch the moon,
the first time I jumped & landed.
The same school where I got my first love note
and the boy told my best friend, having never spoken to me,
he would give her his best Yu-Gi-Oh! card
if I went out with him, as a fair trade. In third grade,

I always brought a pear in a plastic container back to Ms. Myles

from lunch, and she acted surprised every time. The same school

where we built garden beds by the playground

and the net never stayed on the basketball rim longer than twice.

The same school with an etiquette class

where they taught us how to use a tiny fork.

Where state test scores separated the groups in each grade

and all the students pointed about who was in the *smart* groups,

not knowing why in-class segregation split the classroom like the city.

The teachers said *in the name of Maria Montessori*

and you knew you had better

straighten up for some woman who invented education

with your hands. The same school

that gathered us to Pine Mountain in eastern Kentucky and to D.C.,

where the whole class played this hand game

and sang a song my mother taught me.

The same, the same, the same,

where all of us first wrote for red ink proof.

Hot Brown

It's like a turkey BLT with cheese
but deep-fried and with a sauce
no one knows what's in it. At the fair
you can get one on a stick next
to the truck with Krispy Kreme
doughnut cheeseburgers and isn't that
a commentary on health access in Kentucky
or a good sleep afterward. Don't get me
wrong, first it was fancy, but this is not
about how much someone will pay
for something regular but made by a chef
in a hotel ($23), this is about the name
because most of us have not had one
unless you're a tourist, in which case
you are not us. Which is to say,
a Big Red & Grippo's is more Hot Brown
than a billboard Hot Brown
that would probably be best
made with one skillet & spatula
in a kitchen with a ceiling so low

the smoke detector goes siren every time

if it had ever been there (& it hadn't).

Louisville is Also the #1 Producer of Disco Balls in the World (Home to the Last Disco Ball Maker)

It is debatable, so they say, whether or not the cheeseburger was, in fact, invented by Kaelin's Restaurant in Louisville, Kentucky, where it is said to have appeared on menus in 1934. It is also said that while Louisville, Kentucky was the first restaurant to *name* the term cheeseburger, in practice the cheeseburger was experimentally created in Pasadena, California in 1926. In Denver, so they say, the name *cheeseburger* was trademarked in 1935. Of course, while I would like to say that Louisville, Kentucky invented the cheeseburger, it is likely, that in all likelihood, it was invented years and years before in some small kitchen with one cast iron skillet and a gas stove and some woman who wanted more, a table full of children who knew her best. While I cannot truthfully make this more than it is, I would like to say that while Louisville has never been known for poems, poetry is the act of naming, and naming is a call to act and an act in itself, and an act constitutes a thing, and therefore, Louisville invented the cheeseburger and everything before this was solely a hamburger with cheese.

Slant Rhyme Pantoum for Slack Tongue City

Under the Kennedy Bridge the tent city lives the length of drawing blood.

I told you the river never ends.

Since you can only pay insulin or rent, rugged—

if we went missing we never knew until we hit the pavement.

I told you the river never ends

even if we run out of cities to run.

If we went missing we never knew until we hit the pavement.

Because drowning is a well enough way to go,

even if we run (out of cities to run)

we know a few people with seven lives who spared us one.

Because drowning is a well enough way to go,

that is unless we deem an honest coroner.

We know a few people with seven lives who spared us one,

because Augusts are always the hang tide of chaos—

that is unless we deem an honest coroner

who finds, in fact, the moment in which everything goes soft & blurry & heinous.

Because Augusts are always the hang tide of chaos,

this begets the moment in which the tongue lilts, forever—the tongue,

who finds, in fact, the moment in which everything goes soft & blurry & heinous—

Louhʋul, the birth name in which the river fell South & unsung—

this begets the moment in which the tongue lilts, forever—the tongue—

carries all the vowels heavy and slangs the weight slant.

Louhʋul, the birth name in which the river fell South & unsung,

tells you just who grew here and just who came by way of stranger passed.

The Department has released an official statement, resigns

since you can only pay insulin or rent, rugged

old boys with old wealth smoke wealthy fat cigars, watch how at Derby time

under the Kennedy Bridge the tent city lives the length of drawing blood.

A Pegasus[1] was Dismembered Across the Tracks Last Night

after Brigit Pegeen Kelly's "Song"

By noon all the limbs had been taken, the schoolkids beating each other
with the hardened hooves and then tossing them into the bushes.
They sprinted first thing to see it, pointing and throwing
small rocks at the muzzle, their laughter ringing louder than the whine.
The only one quiet, a young girl come dragging a too big lunchbox,
wearing those white church socks with the ruffles. She looked solely
to the ground, head lowered as if her bangs could cover her crying face.
The schoolkids, they teased her, bending down to smile at her tears,
the biggest of them forcing her chin up, raising her small body
and shaking her until she shrieked. In this moment the biggest of them dropped
her and ran, her chin busting open on the metal edge of the lunchbox
as she landed, its contents tossed across the ground. Raising gently,
blood dripping down her chin on her white shirt, she faced the creature, praying
a curse for the hand that drew the knife. The dark and raisined heart,
she wanted to eat it, to invite it someplace warm and alive.
The creature's torso was split down the middle—two limbs at each side like a person.
The wings framed the spilled belly like withered leaves, plucked and dried.
Its bleeding head sat atop the telephone pole just near like a mast, whining

---

[1] References the annual event about which *Inside Louisville* writes, "The Pegasus Parade is the oldest Kentucky Derby Festival event...with floats, inflatables, marching bands, equestrian units, and celebrities."

all night, its long-papered tongue hanging over the side of the big teeth,
mercy to the wind. The eyes glistened whole and unblinking, peering
ahead like a heartwrench, desperate as if to convince reattachment.
Most wicked of all, the heart placed at the front teeth like an apple,
jaw rigid in place. Still, the head's sharp whine pierced
the night through, falling and rising from body memory,
the wind blowing out most of the trill. As for the mane, dry greased
in sweat, the tail below straight as a salute against gravel and rail.
The muscles and sinew were no longer wincing, only the panting face left
to witness its long spine hold its brittle carcass.
At sunbreak the train horn sounded for five minutes straight,
its open throat softer than a siren and more searing to the eardrum.
For those five minutes everyone's stomachs perked their ears
and flipped nausea through and through. If they slept through it
they nightmared only and woke up frantic and jumping. Within the hour,
its open stomach entrails were pasted across every newspaper's face.
That day the city stopped running trains. In its honor,
a yearly parade just before the horses' trumpet call.
Every parade, the girl, she eats hearts, blood dripping down
her chin, chewing every valve until she hears the whine.

On Being From Nobody

The boy who is almost a man comes up to me in the airport at 2 a.m. in his military camouflage and says he missed his flight to Germany. Reeking alcohol and asking for a lighter, he sits next to me and asks me where I'm going. I take a risk—say home, Louisville Kentucky. He slurs *fucking Kentucky? You're from fucking Kentucky? Nobody's from Kentucky.* I say, I've never disliked someone so much within the first 20 seconds of meeting them. He says, let me buy you a drink. I say no. He says do I have to make you. I say no. He says I have to force you. I say no, I am not afraid of you (as in: I am willing to fight death). He says why not. And there is no one else here. I eye the fluorescent exit, its sliding doors into the midnight. I hold my phone in front of my face like a shield, looking for a portal. He tells me I'm not like any girl he's ever met. I say what do you mean. He says *intelligent.* I say that leads me to conclude that you have never met a girl before. And I pray for all the girls and women he has ever met. I reach for silence until the 3 a.m. airport staff arrive, and leave him to find his flight to the country where you can buy a loose cigarette on every corner, so he told me, demanding *wait!* as I escape back. Somewhere there is a military boy who is almost a man telling his military almost men friends about the *intelligent* girl from Kentucky while they laugh, throw a cigarette into the dust and ask for the next joke.

Louisville is Not a Bayou but New Orleans is Its Sister

No, a river is not a swamp but it can get there
in a few days' time by walking. No, we don't have graveyards
beneath every building & enough ghosts to start a war
with angels, or any fear that hurricane season
will cause the cameras to come & witness death breath
by breath. No, we don't have the crawfish
jambalaya étouffée red rice spilled across the picnic table
every season, or the creole Cajun & hot sauce mixed rural.
But, we do know something about water & a railroad
and passed the steamboats down that way for the final
ending. We do have the locals with fleur-de-lis tattooed
on their inner arms & a statue of how the French
first colonized & stamped their footprint in it.
You did bring jazz up from there to mix with folk,
and shotgun houses, of which we built the second most.
We kept our ear to the river & the tracks for the next
you sent, and passed down all word of us in exchange.
One day before I die I'll trace the whole of our childhood
so the mother can see our sister portrait catching light in the front room.

Cave Hill Cemetery

Loyalty gets you killed
but I heard it gets you into heaven first.

In line, the bread loaves never eased the hunger
and at this point we can't separate the unfed

from the gala boys, the cedar box from solid bronze,
and the ground still loosens its jaw all the same.

Here, a land of covered graves, where
if you get a Triple Crown you're immortal

and a bed of roses may buy you a statue
where crowds go to pour bourbon in your name.

For acres, the Confederates lay among the Union,
and this is no tale of romance or post-history,

as surely all of them would have called Ali
out his name—and there he is, still The Prophet

who drove the city East to West in a parade,
all the world's royalty waving next to the vendors

with T-shirts out their trunks you couldn't get anywhere else.
Nowhere else will you see a small Parthenon & bust

erected for fried chicken, though it's more about the Colonel
empire, and the debate here is Indi's vs. Kings, anyway.

Nowhere are more Kentucky bodies stretched,
the nameless amidst the mausoleums,

and all the families shaking their heads,
praying the evidence outlasts them.

Louisville is Kentucky is Mississippi, Too

Though we joke, that Louisville should secede
from Kentucky history, cite our stretched up buildings

and unrural accents, we too must know all the ways
we factory-split the city, mechanical

and mapped just so, red line around the food desert.
Though we would like to think, that we had nothing

to do with plantation old money, are far distant
from the Appalachian Mountains and coal tainted waters

of the east of us, the distillery money that birthed philanthropy,
all the cries of hillbilly & barefoot—we house all the laws of blade.

We took the stage & costumes & TV and are still pointing
look, how much they shout & drawl & live the sticks,

look how much we city & hotel & restaurant our way a republic of lords.
I drove there wayward once to prove it, that we know nothing of the land.

We peer in every South direction, muttering *they take they take they take*,

and still we turn in every circle, asking *anchor me by the neck and not the feet*.

In Which an Entrepreneur is the Mayor

[Louisville, Kentucky]

Once a poet looked to me and said,

I wish my mother had died, so that I would have something to write about.

and I have never been able to turn from it.

Once a city said,

How do we operationalize compassion? before firing 20 bullets into a couple's bed

and never should the masses be able to turn from it.

Each day the tongue grows taller, and now it's almost reached the mouth's roof.

Each day the crowds gather louder, now nearly shaking the first coat of paint off the 2nd St Bridge.

Some days I think about that poet's mother.

I wonder if there is a hum in the gutter that grows to a scream

each time she wishes her daughter a good night's rest.

I imagine all the business meetings scheduled to redraw the city maps,

all the suits smiling slightly as they ask each other which part to cut in two,

how they plot the scalpel mathematically and call this *renaissance*.

This is what a city means,

because the official statement reads [*the city is growing more silent, safer*]

when really it means [*we are casting a mass grave, slowly*]

just like the child poet who likely once told her mother,

[*I'm no good at writing*] when really she meant

[*sometimes I dream of cutting your throat through*].

Reasons of Living There

Lemonade is only made in the South
because the sour that aches your jaw
and makes your head turn can only come from
where the land took in enough salt to slow boil.

My aunt once shouted about okra
in her backyard like a baby was born,
holding the handful above her head
like how kids do first grade drawings.

Trucks last longer because the driver wills
it. Once I saw a calf be born by falling.
Papa doesn't believe in inside dogs. Once
I ate a menu of butter, sugar, and countertops.

The best sausage biscuit I ever had
was from a no-name gas station, wrapped
in thin white with no promise. The puppies
drowned in a water bucket.

If you've handed dry ears of corn
to the cows from a truck bed, their tongues
reaching the full length, you'd know
the concern they might leave nothing left.

It never goes past fall. The pine trees
go unclothed in summer, showing
their small ribs. Every time you reach
for a door, the heat may keep you put.

Magnolia

There's no way out of the South but driving.
Miles of sun.   Good faith
                                                   in an ending.
                    We all know
what last struck the other,
the car window still busted
                    to count who's missing.   Miles of bottles.
A good temper as intimacy.
                                        When the Kentucky man said he might shoot me
                                        for turning around in his driveway
                                               he didn't raise his voice, as by routine.
                                        The last person to lose their way must have unmasked
                                        him, asked *what have you to say*
                                        of yourself? Of your family tree?   Miles of poplar trees.
                    There is a highway no one uses.
                    Towns made for strangers to be lost.
          You'd do scarce to find a mechanic shop with all its parts
or any road without a dead stop.
If you're done enough you'd walk
and somewhere distant

the Dixon

the heat

would bring you to your   knees.   Miles of salt.

Good eating to die quick & well,

the last on your fingers what you stay for.

II.

"It's easier than you thought—leaving."

—Joy Priest

How a Temper Grows Up

In the morning there is a doorway—
bare boned soft feet step bare
so as not to make floorboards scold.

Voices lowered by the dawn,
a small body pressed to the lapel of a kitchen wall,
a cast iron skillet speaking pancake batter.

If I am to be here there must be a blaze,
or at least something that spits and howls
and is not too stubborn to die after burning.

When I learn to love
remind me of the whip between my teeth,
of the bees trapped in my mouth.

Call me home twice like dinner is cold
before I run to beat you
to the place my breath is heaviest.

Though it has not killed me yet,
all I have is red to ward it off.
For safekeeping I repeat,

I have calmed this rage to a rain
you will still smell in your clothes
the morning after.

Every Summer a Garden Hose Made a Pool

and led me to believe maybe metaphors tell
the truth. When the heat rising off the sidewalk
made the trash go rancid, I wrote a new praise

for the man leaning off the garbage truck at the birth
of morning, his orange vest beaming, telling me
he could shoot a basketball good as Kentucky

as I dribbled & fumbled down the alley.
Once my mom told me of Georgia,
I set out in search of a honeysuckle bush

to prove I could be gentle & deft enough to pull
the one drop from the flower just like
she did the days she pushed tire swings

& made peanut butter cookies. I learned
to roller skate on a gym floor & thought
maybe I could crash through a wall

& find a whole other city waiting to tag in once
this one was done & It. We are 7 hours from a coast
in any direction, but somehow I still hear the sea.

Each time I land somewhere, I am reminded there are children
dreaming out of that place just how I did mine.

Ghazal Bedtime Story for Adults

The grown folks swap names at the table,
bow their heads and say grace to the angels.

The young ones fidget, peek glances between prayers,
eyes smirking with angels.

The meal is done, the mimics dull, the plates bathed & dried.
Put to bed, the young ones soften, the ceiling covered in angels.

The grown folks tell The Story, say
the ghosts will quiet, pat their heads, whisper *goodnight, angels*.

The young ones count them off, each drape shadow jumping,
faceless and pulsing, brightening at each laugh for the angel.

The grown folks sleep back to back, see the ghosts
and don't speak, in their nightmares scream *angel!*

The young ones wake crashing, shake the house,
speaking over the rest, say—*dad, I heard you yelling at the angels*.

As a Child I Thought God a Ghost—

a colored robe, water, and the best poetry a psalm could muster.
The draft running through pew to pulpit,

the branch on the window, what kept me awake.
I once ran so far I could name all the hills

on the sole of my shoe and still couldn't catch Him.
They say He sent His prophets to bury us well

and left us all their best poems like a chart to the grave.
Although there was never a prophet who wasn't a poet first

I thought if words were the only flesh there must be one way
to reach Him. I didn't shudder at the howls,

because I thought He was beaming at me. He was never far,
always a silhouette to run through and ask

where all the rest is. All the nights spent shaking,
sleepless, calling for relief—my lips reddened for the dark.

Grief has the least mercy of them all,

so I learned, and to this day I can't say who answers first.

I First Learned of the Girls

When I was 10 I bought a bike for $10 at a yard sale. / I spray painted it white to cover the flowers, / my hands always sticking to the bars. / This was the moment / I dreamed of riding until the wheel burst, / the front bigger than the last, the work / of two young boys with more spares than need. / Each day I journeyed the park, / seeing what I could gather of being still for hours long. / All the couples kissing, they warned me / never came back twice if they were young enough. / To this day I remember the girl, holding the boy's hand, / who winked at me and put a quiet finger to her lips. / I think she must have seen the bike and known, / this was the work of careful signal, / each layer made new when the last faded into bloom.

Ode to Ms. Austin

who carried the school intercom on her belt, the strength
of two principals and a grandma with a glass hairbrush

in her walkie talkie. Who could summon an eclipse such that
you stilled and head bowed at her approach even behind you,

your neck not daring to turn. Rumor was, they modeled megaphones
off her voice, and if you looked directly in her eyes,

the Black Hole would split open and stretch a part
your life's supply of audacity. They say

she made her own lipstick, red from all the children
who lied to her, said they did not throw the first punch

when, in fact, they did, said they did not put ketchup
on the toilet seat, when, in fact, they did—

but she knew this, just wanted you to say it alive once
before she asked you if you did, in fact, love your mother.

She who herself was the first to pilot
the *important* walk down the hallway,

without heels but louder than 1,000 switches,
to arrive at the moment in which she called you

baby, with a wink. Rumor has it, she adopted 12
children, and her house grows a room with each one.

For years I have tried to find her and say thank you,
so that if this poem lands she knows I told the truth,

when on career day she summoned my kindergarten classroom
to ask us what we would be all grown up and finally facing her.

While I Was Small Enough to Pry

To understand my mother, I'd have to run
across a pasture past my breath, among wild dogs
and roosters, feeling my sprinting knees spin

into the wheels of a mad-gone bicycle.
I'd have to tag the base of a tree trunk and look
homeward, smelling spit chewing tobacco and fearing

the looming figure. My mother was my first historian
and still I asked more than she told. Every time she paces
I hear a ringing. I go in search of her childhood,

where the grass spans longer than sound
can carry, bales of hay tucked, ready for the taking.
In her childself's house, the smoke is in the walls

so stubborn it keeps the roof on. If the smoke
sighed, it would all come down. Tension is the only
thing that holds us. And here, an origin strain.

I walk through the door and the ceiling rains.
Before the water is at my calf I taste a banister,
all the years swallowing up like a rainstorm.

If I try to run the mud will rise, the gas stove
will light and rage. Only then can I break apart, know
why she left, drew a veil and kept it ironed.

After the Day My Mother Finds Tied Sheets

My sister rappels down the second story on bed sheets
to find the boy & the fountain where she is safe.

I imagine her a field of dandelions the most common weed
that spreads if you whisper loud. I imagine the boy

a nice one. From the top bunk I play the park swing date
where she always goes higher than him and he smiles.

For breathlessness, they race to the fence hands first,
write dates & *was here* on each other's Chucks for safe keeping.

She laughs, tells me they went to the fountain water
just to throw a fragile thing in and watch it blur.

I listen close through the bunk bed mattress, nights later,
for her muffled sobs. I pray *please please please*

and learn God is a bastard of no bargain.
Still, I offer up all the things I have with a pulse,

know surely this must be sacred enough a trade.
No, this architect's son is not a good one,

not for my sister who first held me
and whispered my name for my soft ears.

All the boys, I curse them, never soft enough to admit it,
how they *cried cried cried* into their pillows' wilted face.

Ode to Adolescent Girlhood

Two girls throw the softball by streetlight. One walked all the way from building S to H for the routine. They test how much each can throw into the dark, what happens if one hits the other. In the parking lot, they eye the cars, daring the other to flinch. One night they drop down on the sidewalk by a wheel because the walking-girl got that feeling like what if water filled all the sky and what will years turn this place into and will you remember me one day sitting on your porch, will you tell somebody's children how you once met a girl who first saw you and you let her. The walked-to girl pitches the softball at a streetlight, watches the moths scatter. She says if we're 40 and ready, I'll marry you and you can tell them yourself.

I Refuse to Believe These are the Best Years

of my life. I would like to think I will be the old woman
with the wheelbarrow full of lavender
and no small talk left in me.
I would like to think I will have a front porch
or at least a stoop to splay myself public
and sitting by my own, maybe no smoke or brown liquor
but enough left to pour to keep them coming by.
I would like to think, that when I smile without my teeth,
there will be no bones left to split in two,
and I will spend my last days pointing, saying *look,*
back across that bend I took the world across my knee.
Look, my daughter, at all the crow's feet
that have gathered right very here to sing her name.
For the ones who told me to drink my 20s straight
because they would be the ripest season of them all,
I hear you can't even break the pit until you're 40
and have no reason left to soft your fangs.
Yes, I swallow sinew, too, and all the children
know me well. Here, my love, come sit with me,
while I map the lightning bugs a path to my open grave.

Ritual of Breathing

My mother works with dying people. She says she can easily
tell, looking in both eyes, who will spend their last nights

scratching, frantically pointing at the corners of the room,
and who will open the door lightly, tilt their heads

and wink just once. She says, near the end, everyone
tugs at their collars, casts their clothes and tries to pull

out of their skins, skeleton and itching. Death, like drugs,
tends to make an honest family, and so they sit in waiting

rooms, saying *I never liked her, but it's nice to see*
a wicked woman still. Or, *remember all the times*

she fought the man for trying to strike us small?
Of course we're all dying people,

but I mean the ones who have the grace and terror
of knowing what's nearest. Sometimes, if they have young

children, they make the chaplain, my mother, tell the children
first, how death means the body means nothing anymore,

how what looks like their mother will soon grow far colder.
Other times, if they have old children,

they make the chaplain, my mother, leave, so the children
can crawl in the bed, place their heads on the collarbone,

their feet hanging off the edge. Once a son went
into the bathroom stall and downed a bottle a tequila,

coming out swaying and asking if it was over yet. No,
it's not over yet. Everything polite dissolves when single

months are left. I always wondered if dying people
cut her off mid-sentence with a head shake if her prayer

didn't salve because their time was especially
too short for limp letters to God. Mostly,

who would be left to know if she did her job badly? She must
have made a sacred pact with everything grim, swore to usher

every last breath true, if only for her own. She must know, when
the heart stops, the chest bursts upward like a sky split endless.

When I Hear of the Mad Women

There is a cave beneath the temple
where all the banished go to gather
to count their rations and smirk
each time they make the ground shake.
Sometimes if I listen close
I can hear them singing, shouting,
the echo of the youngest
ones sharp enough for the taking.
As a girl I talked to them,
thinking how I never felt we were missing
half the world. I watched one lay her head
in the lap of an old woman, the skin
on her hands worked as a winter coat.
In the coldest months they baked pound cake,
feeding each other as a gift. They always sang
with their chins upward, pushing another flower up
through the mud with each chorus.
At my turning point one pushed me away,
summoning my mother
to see if she had other children

calling for severance from this earth city before their time.

Still, I know them.

The same way I know the happiest I've seen my mother

and all her women friends were the nights they told the stories,

laughing until they hurt, ending *God, remember when we met!*

Wishes That Keep Me

If I find a field of rye I'll tell how I spent it all

even before I had the nerve. I could make my mother live

forever but then she would be the only one left

when the sun turns coal. Once I took a string

and traced my walk from the front door

and still sometimes I leave my maps out in the rain.

Do you know train tracks

are man-made rivers, all through here?

Today, when the refrigerator spits up the river

I won't wonder how the house flooded

starting from the attic. For once, I slip

and let it take me, down to where the fire

hydrants grow their heads new each summer day.

If the weeds dry up first then I know the glass

will be last, its pane still head-high as it bends

elastic. The next man I find with a knife

I'll ask for the nearest memory of when he last held

his sister close. If I spend my life trying

to open my mouth big as the night

I won't have to spend the rest counting

the days I didn't run the ocean whole.

Some days I think there must be a richer color

I have never seen—there must be a mine

buried beneath the holler waiting for us to finish

so that it may speak. I'm listening,

and it took a near death to bring me here.

I come back home, looking for something

I found years ago but can't hold still.

Night Truths That Keep Me From Ripping My Collar

It is instinctual to seek isolation before death

therefore I have an explanation.

I have a theory honey can cure everything.

To be exact is to lie.

I don't believe in straight women.

There is someone somewhere singing while cooking.

The practice of using euphemisms is to avoid invitation.

If I name all the worst, I can make my way to morning

and have already passed them all.

When Everything is Desperate

I find the women who till their hearts so much
      that death is just a phase.
I answer then, to them with well-water eyes

and something to show for their shoulders. Who say,
      My name is whoever speaks first and doesn't shrink.
These record women, with their chests open,

      have smiled past the corners
for too many years to put in albums.
      Their tales low and lighter fluid, childhoods spent sprinting

      for the hills. Ah, when they slow
dance, I see the wolf pick,
      and they tell me it's all burning anyway.

      If the apocalypse comes first,
I'll have their faces in mind until the last lightning
      when God herself will blink.

      When summer comes I'll ask my grief,
have all four seasons spent you yet?

Counting the Attic

Three vases, a black-eyed Susan, and a pocket watch.
For the time being the pane is clean—
I spend days up here collecting everything
I'd most rather be caught with at my last,

taking inventory of all my small good things:
Once a beet grew out of the garden
dirt though I never planted it.
Sometimes after a shower

I glisten, not knowing how
long I can stand the bare.
I've never played an instrument
because I feared it would swallow

me soundless.
I rarely walk with anyone
and I have no sorrow for the solitude of trees.
—A pine branch, two glasses, and a whistle.

I smirk knowing no one can find me here, the house
still happening beneath my figure splayed on the floor.

My Mother Had Hands Before She Had Children

after John Murillo's "Hustle"

Mom said she made her back bad from those hands,
raised three children plus her siblings with those hands.

Left the country and all its gins and rain hymns—
made a house from a paycheck with those hands.

Took a paint can and a ladder to a gutter,
made a garden from dirt and seed with those hands.

I told her once, *I've seen angels on the ground*,
while she turned a bathtub faucet with those hands.

She's seen angels on the ground, too, ones with skin
and teeth and fingers that reach like with those hands.

Said a prayer and lit a daily candle,
burned wicks for peace with those hands.

Used to wade in rivers and bike fast as red,
pick peaches high as clouds with those hands.

For her first born she planted a magnolia tree
in the front yard, sturdy as a pillar from those hands.

She tells me, *when it's time, I want my ashes spread,*
so I can touch everything again with those hands.

I tell her I'll do it twice—I'll run smooth as water
and still I'll eat because of those hands.

Song from the Color Red

The spit from a chicken's neck,
the aftertaste of a busted lip,
what's left to bathe in when the water runs out,
the only color that howls & rings.

The stain in her jeans,
the womb made casket,
the butcher's outstuck tongue,
what the wood can't unabsorb.

The trumpet's downpour,
the lover's studying of sheets & bleach,
the parted sea,
what the walls were painted afterward.

All that's left, the wrath, the stirred,
the gash over the doorway,
the spill that beckons the washing,
the deep clean, loud & heard.

The slaughter's genesis & afterword,

the lollipop after the needle,

the handshake truce,

carved in the tree trunk.

Biography of a [   ] Girl

She is derivative of a shovel, a switchblade, and a blue gourd. She has no grammar for death. She calls for God and God lefts. She likes the feeling of being spent. She knows only that her guardian came from glory. Run, tell the hills of her heavy breath. She spends herself pacing. She spends her friends silent, sitting. She takes the stairs two at a step. She weeps at her tale, how anonymous her beginning. She calls forth her choir, their swaying outrage. Run, tell the others of her grieving. She rests her soreness, all its ills. She spins. She circles. She rounds the cycle of her rising chest. She turns her insides out and her face reds. She sinks a whale and it gives. She feasts, leashes the belly. She spoils and the levee gives. Run, tell how her name never ends—

Prayer List

Send me torn chicken feathers, two matches, and no kerosene.

      Send me ancient.

Send me a sore throat and all the leeches.   Send me reckless.

Send me a bayou and nowhere to put the water.

For once, send me distilled perfumes. Send me a wooden box

      full of hay and one emerald brooch,

        send me a thousand tongues cut from the mouth of one hyena.

                      Send me home.

Then leave me there.

I found you sobbing at all the ugly, remember? Send me empty

      cans with strings so I can walk them down the street as my leashed dog.

Send me defeated.

Send me cowering at your waist.

Send me ten nectarines that I can pitch against the fence and

      scream when they don't break. Send me empty.

Send me a math book. So I can refuse to do one more thing.

Mail me a highway and ask if I've swallowed it yet—sometimes

I catch all the mice you missed by the tail and chew them slowly

      to be fair, so their small paws twitch down my cheeks.

Send me all the cicadas the underground has to offer,

so I can drum as they wail the mass chorus in my ear.

Send me all your nightmares, so I can compare notes.

Send me all the letters I've ever saved and burn them right in front of me—

this one last time, send me devastated and call me honest.

III.

"I write poems because I can't sing."

—Amaud Jamaul Johnson

On the Day I Bury the River

I wear white lace to mourn
because I can cut it between my teeth.

I take an axe just in case. The coffin is so heavy
the pallbearers drag it—the river's limbs and its body.

It screams so loud a tree falls. It claws the wood.
It hounds. It heavy breathes and says my name.

It shoulders against the lid to find the opening.
They bury it with concrete because it first escaped

the dirt. For 90 days it starved and never once died.
Most times I am hungry it eats my stomach.

When they chained the casket shut its arm snapped.
Every time I walk it moves the ground beneath me.

Every willow tree I see mourns me. In the sunrise
the first I notice—how everything is winter dead.

I leave the service shaking, my lips bleeding—

Oh, how a funeral spills from the parlor.

On Heavy

All these days I have sat with my stone heart   and it still raises a riverbed

each nighttime.   I use this stone heart to pound the stains from my washing

and glance past my shoulder at the bench where we laid   our insides woven.

I use this stone heart to weigh my chest a wingspan   like when I opened

and showed you   all my good light.   I use this stone heart to sink.

My heart is a puddle   I learn from   all it does is stretch and ache.

After I Have Shown You All My Worlds & Now Your Shadow is in All of Them

On the days I spend most my time praying

I don't run into someone I recognize

I am to the brim and the rest of me waits

for the spill. I bring the band in my pocket

in case I need the shouting and I do.

There is no public sidewalk that allows safe sitting

but I consider it, to be low

to the ground and not have to look

anything in the eye. On these days

I find a tree, though it's not a willow,

and carve until the wind breaks.

Pantoum for Rain in the South

I try not to cry in public.
I can't stay anywhere it never hot rains.
I stand at the foot & fight the ocean.
Find you waiting, eyes sad but uncried.

I can't stay anywhere it never hot rains,
my clothes hanging in drawl—
find you waiting, eyes sad but uncried.
I pray & hold with you there,

my clothes hanging in drawl.
This is when the sand quicks & caves me in.
I pray & hold with you there—
you leave to light the candle before the tide comes.

This is when the sand quicks & caves me in.
I yield the endings that surround me, how they empty.
You leave to light the candle before the tide comes—
the mirror strikes me, its unending sharpness.

I yield the endings that surround me, how they empty.
You say the beast is most hungry in the early morning.
The mirror strikes me, its unending sharpness.
You tell me the belly has you in full now.

You say the beast is most hungry. In the early morning,
I stand at the foot & fight the ocean—
you tell me the belly has you in full now.
I try not to cry in public.

I Don't Know Which Memories I Have Permission To

I tell her *strip me from the inside*—
my shields spill,
armor bows at her feet.
She renders me skinless,
an open wound. She presses
the opening—her mouth.
The blood holds, waits
for her palm to stomach.
It withers, my pit bellows
and squints. My knees catch,
my head begs her navel—
I limp. I fall vacant.
I ask her, *make dust of me.*
The darkness spins, faints.
My throat digs, drinks.
All night we spend pacing,
trying to pin the other
and hand back everything that fell.

Portraits of Lush

My most remarkable lie is that I never wanted to play the music so loud the limes burst. My chin raised and eyes closed to dissolve into a breaking. I did, in fact, want to be both the stage and the disappear. I did, in fact, want the solitude of the lone trumpet and the choir of the tambourines. I did, in fact, worry that one day I may end up in a big empty house, and worry that I may like it. Or that I may build a pine with someone and spend the best of my back ripping it down, bark by biting bark. Or worse, pass by it every day as it raises limb by reaching limb. In fact, we parted before anything spoiled and that is the grand ending, how the sun flicked out at our bright blue meridian. Like a tomato growing age in the sun, skin peeling off from the wrinkle, revealing the blush heart beneath. Here, on my porch, a crate of easily bruised peaches, the gayest fruit. They rot so sweet but never burst, sleeping down into the grass, staining my outside shoes.

I Must Confess I Still Believe in Romance

I.

She asks me why I write love poems
and I say because I want to document the world ending.
Though I filled myself with honeybees until the rupture,
I would do it all again so that my stomach drops
the cliff. When finally, our self-destruction takes the hill,
and we set oil to the water ablaze, I want to sit with you
on the stoop swing, saying how the sunset dropped
to the ground and somersaults even wilder
than we thought. When the trumpets call for blood
I want you to tell me what you hear while I listen
to your chest beat for the proof. While the last
of the troops take the tanks against God,
I want to debate, rolling in the grass, if the sky
is more boundless than the whole of the earth ground
that curves into new each day. Despite the wrecking,
I want to have my math right, so I can tell the angels
just how many and just how tall. Despite the slowing

room I want to climb the depth of you, so that

when I say *the end* the staircase laughter doesn't cease.

II.

I must confess I still believe in romance.
Before I cried out all the blue I found
the most wonderful well where the hymn flew,
the bottom dropping lower with each new wish.
If I knew you before, the way my stomach washboards
could have cast me through, soft enough to draw
you out where I bent wind to your name. In April,
before I waited to call the first spring after you,
I could have raised a riverbed truer than the last.
When we danced the rooftop to the ground floor
I knew again how women bite the root. Before
I threw my levees out I summoned three limbs
and a beating heart to tell me when to cease.
Yes here we built a tree, laughing as we rounded
the belly, telling how maple sap thickens the tongue
and then the leaves. I found you, don't you remember?
How quickly a woman loves a woman
and then has to bury it alive.

III.

I must confess I still believe in romance.

Of all the genocides we tell our children before bed

this one has no softness but in the grief hum.

See, I saw a girl hand me her best memory

and therefore I still believe in her.

I watch us watch museums of massacre

and then stumble out into the dry air,

clean of the scalps but reeking of them,

and I reach for a rocking chair

or something I can fall into. For once,

I see my father cry in public and I believe him,

all the times he watched movies about fathers dying.

When I rest, I think of all the times my breath

has stopped and if I could fly without all my teeth.

See, of all the dinner tables eating silent

there is a family rage so shaking the music starts

and so this time I pass the salt.

When I leave here, I want to meet all the women

with best memories they still have

and gather us in until she is full.

Fat as we are, I eat the rest, for of all the butchers,

she is the sharpest, even as she sleeps.

America, how endless and dying,

have we no want for heaven at all?

Thank You

Louisville, thank you for raising me. This had to be my first book. To all who witnessed and passed through Young Poets of Louisville, thank you for gathering in the name. Hajjar Baban, Mackenzie Schubert, India Sada, Michael Lee, thank you for reading and giving feedback on some of the poems here. Natasha Oladokun, thank you for reading the first of it. Amaud Jamaul Johnson, thank you for your teaching and your wisdom. Joy Priest, thank you for bringing the city with you. Amaris, your love sees me through.

I bid my gratitude to the team at Sundress for their precious attention to build this house for these poems.

Notes

Section break I, pg. 15, quote is from "Finding Transcendence in the Living and Dead" by Melena Ryzik, published in *The New York Times* on February 1, 2013.

"Sestina for Louisville Jug Band Music," pg. 26, quote is from Michael Jones' *Louisville Jug Music* where he also wrote, "Louisville is considered the home of jug music because it produced the first jug band to record in the studio."

"My Elementary School Was Named After a Poet," pg. 29, includes a reference to "The Red Wheelbarrow" by William Carlos Williams.

"In Which An Entrepreneur is the Mayor," pg. 44, the quote 'How do we operationalize compassion?' is sourced from Mayor Greg Fischer in the podcast entitled "The Nation's First Compassionate City?" released through *In the Arena: A Governing Podcast*, published June 25, 2018.

Section break II, pg. 51, quote is from Joy Priest's "American Honey."

Section break III, pg. 91, quote is from a lecture during ENGL 207 Introduction to Creative Writing at the University of Wisconsin-Madison in Fall 2016.

About the Author

Mackenzie Berry is from Louisville, Kentucky. Her poetry has been published in *Vinyl, Up the Staircase Quarterly, Hobart,* and *Blood Orange Review,* among others. A graduate of the University of Wisconsin-Madison through the First Wave Program and Goldsmiths, University of London, she is pursuing an MFA in Poetry at Cornell University.

Other Sundress Titles

Mouths of Garden
Barbara Fant
$12.99

To Everything There Is
Donna Vorreyer
$12.99

Something Dark to Shine In
Inès Pujos
$12.99

Hood Criatura
féi hernandez
$12.99

Cosmobiological
Jilly Dreadful
$16.99

Sweetbitter
Stacey Balkun
$12.99

Slaughter the One Bird
Kimberly Ann Priest
$12.99

I Am Here to Make Friends
Robert Long Foreman
$14.99

The Valley
Esteban Rodriguez
$12.99

nightsong
Ever Jones
$12.99

What Nothing
Anna Meister
$12.99

Maps of Injury
Chera Hammons
$12.99

www.ingramcontent.com/pod-product-compliance
Lightning Source LLC
Chambersburg PA
CBHW081418090426
42738CB00017B/3414